Reflections in a Boomer's Eye

Poems and Musings

M.L. VanBlaricum

Reflections in a Boomer's Eye

M.L. VanBlaricum

Snap Brim Press

Santa Barbara, 2016

Reflections in a Boomer's Eye
Poems and Musings

Copyright © 2016 by Michael L. VanBlaricum
All rights reserved

Cover and book design by Maddie Rose Maranto
Author photo provided courtesy of ECE Illinois

Enquiries to:
SnapBrimPress@gmail.com

First Edition, thus – February 2016
Originally published in September 2015
as a private limited edition.

Published by
Snap Brim Press
PO Box 874
Goleta, CA 93116

ISBN: 978-0-9967684-2-9

For my parents, Glenn and Mary Ellen VanBlaricum, who, in 1950, made me a Boomer.

Contents

Random Walks

Sentimental Over You

Boom

Postscript

Notes

Acknowledgements

About the Author

Preface

I grew up in an era when schools generally did everything they could to turn students off of poetry. Of course, they thought they were doing just the opposite. But being made to memorize a poem that didn't speak to you or learning the "meaning" of a poem as the teacher had learned it in college have never been effective ways of introducing students to poetry. I distinctly remember arguing with my college prep English teacher about the meaning of a T.S. Eliot poem. My interpretation was wrong and the teacher's was right. Exasperated, I finally asked her if she knew the poet and had asked him directly what he was trying to say. I was given a B in that class.

Fortunately, my dad (a history teacher and my grade school principal) liked poetry and would recite a few lines on the appropriate occasions. Poems with lines like:

> *The sun that brief December day*
> *Rose cheerless over hills of gray,*
> *And, darkly circled, gave at noon*
> *A sadder light than waning moon.*
> *Snow-Bound: A Winter Idyll* by John Greenleaf Whittier

> *The golden-rod is yellow;*
> *The corn is turning brown;*
> *The trees in apple orchards*
> *With fruit are bending down.*
> *September* by Helen Hunt Jackson

At the same time, my mother sang around the house a lot. She inadvertently taught me songs with lines like:

"Hut-Sut Rawlson on the rillerah and a brawla, brawla sooit,"

The Hut-Sut Song (a Swedish Serenade) by Leo V. Killion,
Ted McMichael, Jack Owens

"This ole house once rang with laughter
This ole house heard many shouts
Now he trembles in the darkness
When the lightnin' walks about."

This Ole House by Stuart Hamblen

and, the most poignant of all:

"Boop boop diten datem whatem choo
And they swam and they swam back over the dam."

Three Little Fishies by Saxie Dowell

I was usually too busy blowing things up in our basement or building contraptions in our backyard to give much thought to what I was hearing. I focused my energies on science, math, and ultimately on engineering and girls. However, the descriptions, words, and rhythms my parents presented are still with me.

I will admit that during the summer of 1970 I listened to Franklyn MacCormack's Meister Brau Showcase on WGN at eleven o'clock at night. He interspersed moody, contemplative music with poetry. He opened his show reading Mary Carolyn Davies' poem "Why Do I Love You" with Wayne King's orchestra playing Hans Engleman's 'Melody of Love' in the background:

Why do I love you?
I love you not only for what you are, but for what I am when I am with you. I love you not only for what you have made of yourself, but for what you are making of me. I love you for ignoring the possibilities of the fool in me . . .

Schmaltzy? Yes! But it did have an impact on me as a nineteen year-old who had a lot of possibilities of the fool in him.

I will also admit that I have always enjoyed the trochaic pentameter rhythms of Longfellow's *The Song of Hiawatha*.

> *By the shores of Gitche Gumee,*
> *By the shining Big-Sea-Water,*
> *Stood the wigwam of Nokomis,*
> *Daughter of the Moon, Nokomis.*

Not to mention the Hamm's Beer jingle.

> *From the Land of Sky Blue Waters*

My wife is from Nokomis so clearly there was some sort of subliminal message I got from Mr. Longfellow.

When I was thirty I became interested in writing. However, at that time, I was focused on mysteries and thrillers (you know, Dan Fortune, Lew Archer, and James Bond). Poetry was not something I considered writing until I turned sixty and started to contemplate my existence. At that time my attention span became very abbreviated due to a short circuit in my head so poems, essays, and sundry musings were things I could finish before a squirrel ran by or I was distracted by a bright shiny object. I also thought it was about time that I learned to express what I was feeling, what I was seeing, or what I was remembering in words.

This brief book is a compilation of a few of the writings I have put on paper over the past five years. I have tried to reflect and focus on the experiences of my life as a Boomer. I was born in 1950 and graduated from high school and started college in the explosive year of 1968. I have lived in seven decades (or eight depending on how you count), two centuries, and two millenia. Therefore, I think

I qualify as a prototypical Boomer. Hence, in this collection, there are memories of teenage angst as well as other reflections on my first thirty years of life. However, this writing is certainly not limited to reminiscences of my early life. There are some musings and observations on experiences from my age of baldness here as well. My hope is that at least one line plucks a nerve or a heart string of my gentle readers.

Ray Bradbury once said in a class I was in that we should write all the junk about the baggage of our lives and get it out of the way first so we can really start to write in earnest. Perhaps this is my attempt to follow Mr. Bradbury's advice.

Boomers

Internal Dialogue #1

I don't get it … said the engineer.
Feel it   … said the poet.

It doesn't sound reasonable.
The heart doesn't need reason.

So I should forget what my brain tells me?
Yep!

But I like logic.
Use it to find your words.

The language is different
Learn a new one of image and sound.

I like formulas.
Emotions become thoughts, thoughts become words.

Engineers get ideas and build on them.
So do poets.

I mean like building a bridge.
Exactly, spanning two sides of an idea over raging uncertainty.

The Wolf Moon

Out the window of the bus,
from O'Hare to my childhood,
I watch the full Moon rise
over snowy,
cornstalk-stubbled fields.

The luminous orb of night,
the return to my roots,
and the freedom of age,
unburden my senses.

Now at its apex
the moon,
unshrouded by the glow
of my artificial securities,
allows vision in the darkness.

A tidal wave
of emotions,
rekindles cravings,
and awakens
the werewolf of my psyche.

I sniff the winds of my youth,
and remember
thrills in the moonlight,
latent aspirations,
and loves lost.

Vintage Friend

In the dust
And cobwebs
Of my cellar,
I find an old friend.

I remember my first encounter;
A beautiful label beckoned,
A varietal I admired,
From a vintner near home.

Alas, the date declared her youth;
I chose to leave her untouched
To mature on her own.

Life moved on;
I experienced other wine,
Some sparkling,
Others dry and hollow.

I now cautiously approach her;
Will age cause her to be acidic?

Or will she be mature,
With a multi-layered bouquet?

I partake.
She is full bodied and sweet
With a smooth, yet complex finish.

September 1968
Freshman Year - New Student Week

"O the joy of my spirit – it is uncaged – it darts like lightning!"
From "A Song of Joy," by Walt Whitman

Off to the Big U.

Freedom is mine.

I can get up when I want,
Eat what I want,
Come in when I want,
Go to bed when I want,
With whomever I want.

But …
Best of all

No one knows me.

Think About It

By definition
All the parents of Baby Boomers
Survived World War Two.

Are we Boomers,
Therefore,
A selective breed?

Boomers

Children of the Greatest Generation.
What does that make us?

Far out?

The Nature of Things

After the First Hard Frost

The sycamore
With her alabaster limbs
Outstretched to the clear
Azure sky
Stands disrobed
With only
       Dangling, red Converse All Stars
             once worn in a winning game;
       Squirrels' dreys
             made of last summer's leaves
             hiding a winter stash;
       And the skeleton of Sally's first kite,
To protect her modesty.

January in Illinois

It is well below freezing,
The air is translucent gray,
The world is dusted by snow sprites.

Outside my frost-fractaled window
A robin sits on a pine branch,
A junco sits
On my ice fringed skylight,
My wife sits in California
Playing with our grandchildren,
All daring me to come out and play.

A Question of Nature

How do birds build their nests?
How do they start?
How do they hold
      That first
             twig,
             leaf,
             or string,
      In place
While they fly away to get another?

A Noisy Thanks

So far this spring, in my 'hood, I've seen:
Intrepid black crows cawing and mean,
Lazy red-tailed hawks soaring to maul,
Energetic woodpeckers dominating all,
Nascent black phoebes in their nest of three,
Tiny Anna's hummingbirds swooping with glee;

Scrub jays behaving as if they're king,
Pairs of mourning doves each pitying,
Robins, red-breasted, digging my grubs,
Ignoble house sparrows filling the shrubs,
Northern mockingbirds acting like barons,
Gopher-stalking great blue herons;

Rufous hummingbird being a missile,
A charm of gold finches eating our thistle,
California towhees gleaning the heather,
House finches in their varied red feathers,
Elusive bluebirds delivering peace,
Large band-tailed pigeons looking obese;

Citrine hooded orioles, exotic,
A pair of quail, almost quixotic,
Radiant and showy black-headed grosbeak,
Sets of mallards away from their creek,
Oak titmice with their Mohawks frenetic,
Nuthatch, white breasted, looking ascetic.

Icicles

Stalactites
On the edge of the house,
Some carrot fat, others pencil thin,
Some long, some short,
Some solo, others in chorus,
All cold.
Dripping
Rhythmically into the snow.
Formed by melting sun and freezing air
Together.
How long before they grow too long, too heavy,
And their connection breaks?
Can
These glistening
Columns really fall and spear my head?
We sucked on them as kids – a poor kid's winter Popsicle.
Good thing we didn't have acid rain,
Or, did we?
People
In California put lighted ones up at Christmas.
Seems silly but maybe there is
A desire for the real thing,
A fascination.
Icicles.

Petit Gris

I rise early, walk to the driveway to get the Times; the dew from the morning coastal fog is on the grass. A brown garden snail scurries across the sidewalk to the safety of the bushes after spending the night eating my amaryllis. Not a scurry by people standards, but in her mind she is doing a sprint. I call her Tove. I watch her slither, gyre, and gimble towards the boxwood.

I used to stomp snails or throw them into the street to take their chances dodging cars. I now carefully pick up the slithy Tove and carry her gently to my backyard. I place her in front of my Eastern box turtle, Duchess, who is currently enjoying the wabe. Duchess loves Petit Gris Escargot, but she is not an elegant eater.

To A Hoppy Toad

You come out at dusk,
As the lightning bugs materialize,

Camouflaged until you hop
Overtop our verdant lawn.

Hunting with patience,
To clear the grass of insects.

I sneak up behind you.

You jump forward
Into my outstretched hands

And pee on me.

The old folks say I'll get warts.
I don't care.

If I do,
Grandma Dessie will rid them with
A bean, an apron pocket, and an incantation.

A Turtle in a Tree

Let me make this simple decree
I've never seen a turtle in a tree.

Why do you think that might be?
Is it nature, or is it just me?

I've seen many bugs up in trees,
Including butterflies, beetles, and bees.

I've seen all kinds of birds, of course
And a paratrooper from the Air Force.

I even saw two bears one day
And once, I saw a Chevrolet.

Many a cat
Occasionally a rat

A beautiful kite
Grabbed in flight

Squirrels of every color and stripe
A raccoon family running in fright

A house built by the neighbor kids
From boards, old doors, and garbage can lids.

Once I saw a lumber jack
And a Cub Scout with a yellow pack.

I've seen turtles on land and sea
But never, ever, up a tree.

Racing the Rain

I remember one
Bright, sunny, Illinois July day
When I was fourteen.

Even though the sky was blue and the sun was shining,
The maple trees started flipping their leaves
To show their silver linings.

A north wind started to blow.
We heard the screams of neighbor kids,
The northern sky darkened.

Then we saw our friends
Running down the middle of the street
Shrieking with laughter.

Right behind them was a downpour.
The younger, slower kids were drenched.
The older faster ones were one step ahead of the deluge.

We joined the rank of harbingers
And ran ahead of the drencher
Until the storm was tired of our children's game, and
Soaked us all to the bone.

Christmas

Winter looms

Family gathers

Warmth ensues

The Nature of Things

The white-spotted, pale-brown fawn
Who last Sunday feasted on our new cabbage and pepper plants,
Who teased our beagle, Dixie, to the end of her chain,
Who bounded playfully into the safety of the woods
Whenever we drove into the driveway,
Is lying near the side of the gravel road;
The maggots are using her body the way she used our garden.

Moon Shadows

Off Cartagena
In the Crow's Nest Lounge of the ms Maasdam

Hypnotized by the white capped Caribbean Sea
I look to the clouds for respite.

Alas,
The cumulus,
Are nebulous.

I was hoping to find
        A Bokhara carpet flying high,
        A genii emerging from her lamp,
        A five-toed dragon breathing fire,
        A leprechaun with his pot of gold,
        And a mermaid singing her siren's song.

But wait …
        There's a tortuga,
        And a three-toed sloth,
        A pirate's skull
            with two bones crossed,
        A piranha
            with its razor teeth
        And a very happy flying fish.

Shape shifters all.

The Lucky One

As I ate my lunch on the fenced-in boardwalk of Lincoln Park

A momma mallard and her brood of nine
Marched proudly past in a line

Then momma broke the file
and nudged her issue toward the fence
Three squeezed through a hole
And plunged into the lilypad pond

Then two more followed suit

Momma duck, now anxious
Paced back and forth
Quacking guidance

Two more went in

The final two were obstinate
Or afraid
But surely not of the water

I looked over the fence
Seven baby ducks were huddled
Peeping and looking for the source
Of their momma's frantic quacking

One more took the plunge

Momma duck
Leaving number nine behind
Flew over the fence
And joined her paddlings
To keep them safe

The lone duckling wandered and peeped her desperation
A nearby golden retriever eyed her
As did a crow with hunger in its eyes

I set down my sandwich,
Joined a mother with a stroller, and
Shooed the frenetic straggler to safety

The mother, turning to her son in the stroller, said,
"You are lucky you are not one of nine."

Epistle

Today, I wrote a letter —
      the kind you fold,
            place in an envelope,
          address,
              and post.

Alas,
      These days
      No need to lick the stamp.
      A personal way to finalize a letter —
A kiss.

I prefer handwritten missives.
I can tell from the lines,
      the stroke,
         the angle,
            the size of the script,
The writer's mood:
      Hurried,
         Mad,
      Harried,
         Sad.

Sometimes coffee stains the paper,
Sometimes tears.
        No emoticons are needed.

I had a girlfriend
who perfumed her letters;
        My Sin!
What that did to a seventeen year old boy –
        Elysian emotions.

A real letter costs:
        paper,
                an envelope,
                                a stamp,
And a trip to the nearest mailbox.

The wait for a reply can be torture.
Did the courier make it through?
Was the letter stayed by rain or snow
Or gloom of night?
Or worse,
Stayed by the reader.

Trying to Relax on a Summer's Day

I sit in my chaise lounge.

The phone rings.

I let my recorded voice
Say, "We're not home …"
While I enjoy
the hummingbird
        sucking nectar
from the blue columbine.

A monarch lands on our milkweed
to lay her eggs.

The doorbell rings;
        I didn't know it worked.

I get up and go to the door;
        It could be my wife
        with an armful of groceries.

There stands an
old hippie lady
with dirty-blond braids,
leather headband,
and purple batik dress.

Could I tell her which house
had a garage sale last weekend?

I'm sorry,
we were not home last weekend.

Sorry to bother.
They had a fly fishing kit
and I have a friend who's into fly fishing.

We were not home last weekend.

Sorry.
Does the man who lives next door
have a lot of tools in his garage?

My neighbor
is a 97 year old widow.

Sorry to bother you.

I return to my yard.

The monarch
and hummingbird
are still working their plants.

The hooded oriole on the fence
stares at the empty feeder,
looks my way,
and chirps its demands.

Uncle Lester

When telling his many stories,
he sat with his elbows on his knees,
stared straight at the ground,
And poked it with a stick.

His farm was a playground:

A three-hole outhouse for,
        Papa, mama, and baby butts.
        Complete with a Sears-Roebuck catalog.

A *Wizard of Oz* like storm cellar
        Where Aunt Effie stored
        canned tomatoes and peppers.

A garden and greenhouse of exotic plants.

A collection of Shawnee arrowheads and ax heads.

A freezer full of rabbit and squirrel.

But mostly, a yard with an abundance of toads.
        Hoppy toads my aunt called them.

We asked Uncle Lester why he always looked down
'Watching the ants at work,' was his answer.

The March of Time

The frost was on the pumpkin as
The Princeton High School Band
Lined up in Darius Miller Park
For the annual Thanksgiving parade
Down the crowd lined Main Street.

I drank the free Lion's Club hot cocoa,
Trying not to burn my tongue,
Then moved to my position in the front line.

I blew into my mouthpiece to keep it warm.

Janie, with her silver baton,
And her blue sequined leotard,
Lined up directly in front of me.
Her bare legs made me curious
About her warmth.

She turned and approached,
         Girls didn't generally approach trombone players.
She smiled and asked,
Would I put her watch in my pocket while we marched?

March I did,
         warmly.

Rorschach Test
Winter of 2014, Urbana, Illinois

A single icicle,
as thick as my thumb,
sparkling like a crystal dagger,
    hangs off the black running boards
    of my red salt-covered 4-Runner.

Will it fall off
    at home,
    at the Spurlock Museum,
    on Green Street,
or, perhaps, the ice-rink?

Two days pass —
It picks up road grime,
and hangs on tenuously
like the finger of a fire-charred skeleton.

Day three —
It is thinner.
Age is taking its toll.

The fourth day —
It falls in my driveway, and
cracks into three pieces;
its translucent core
sparkles in the rare sunlight.

Now —
Smashed
by my tire
it is

A broken spirit.

Moon Shadow

My wife watches Masterpiece Theatre; I sit alone, relaxing in our hot tub. The full December Moon is directly overhead. Jupiter, the red Betelgeuse, and a few bright stars in the blue velvet sky are brilliant in the calm, cold air. The critters are silent — no rats scurrying in the purple Mexican sage, no raccoons walking through the pernicious bamboo, no hooting of the owls in the nearby eucalyptus grove.

Saturated with serenity, I move to climb out. A large black shadow appears on the bottom of the bath. The water is transparent in the moonlight. The surface is still. No ambiguity about the shadow; it is not mine. Something is between me and the moon. Close, really really close. It grows larger with time – coming for me. Yet, I hear nothing. Could it be the angel of death? At dinner I stuffed my arteries on a four course Italian meal complete with tiramisu and Ruffino Chianti. I feel fine — no chest pains, no jabbing head pains, no double vision.

Then, I remember the great horned owl's ability to attack in the dark in total silence. My bald head with its band of gray hair moving slowly across the tub could look like prey.

The shadow increases in size, I look up, exposing my eyes to whatever is coming for me. A large black body is ten feet above me. It sees me and escapes silently into the shadows of the ficus tree. What if I had not detected its shadow? What if it had struck? Would its raptor talons grab my ears and pull? What if it was the angel of death?

Random Walks

Why You No Longer See Teeter Totters in Playgrounds

Now and again,
I meet someone
I want to hold at the top
of a Teeter Totter;

With my feet
Solidly on the ground
I would bounce a little
To let them know their plight,
Then, step off and walk away.

Orange is an Easy Rhyme

They say
You can't rhyme orange,
         the color.
Which means you can't rhyme orange,
         the fruit.

Orange is made of
Red plus yellow.

I can rhyme red.
         and,
I can rhyme yellow.

So rhyming orange is not
An odd bed-fellow.

Today I Found

Two cents
Two dirty coppers
Two pennies

Do two people want my thoughts?
Do I get twice as much luck?
        Or …
May I have two days' worth?

The Vision

In an upstairs
Blue-framed window
Of a gray boarding house
With her sunrise lit emerald eyes
Fixed on the distant skies
She brushes the auburn hair
flowing over her tanned shoulders.

She seems oblivious to the fact that she is
Standing
In an upstairs
Blue-framed window
Of a gray boarding house
Naked.

She doesn't seem to care
That she is on display,
In an upstairs
Blue-framed window
Of a gray boarding house
Like Venus rising.

Maybe the rain
Or the hour
Make her feel safe.
Maybe she is drunk,
Or high on life.

Perhaps
She knows
Exactly what she is doing
In an upstairs
Blue-framed window
Of a gray boarding house.

I'm glad I picked this morning
To start jogging again.
Exercise certainly pays off.

Never to Know for Sure

For the better part of a year,
     For a few days,
He studied her closely,
     From a distance.
She invited him in
     But never opened up,
Only willing to reveal
     Her external beauty.

A Cold Day in July

My dad, a Cardinals baseball fan, always said:
"The coldest day I ever saw
was a July day in the stands of Wrigley Field."

I assumed his experience was due to the lake effect.
Wrigley sits only a few blocks from frigid Lake Michigan
Where the icy cold winds coming off of the lake
Are a mainstay
Even on a hot summer's day.

But after fifty-five years of thinking about it,
I now realize
It was because the Cubs beat the Cards that day
And hell froze over a little.

Random Walks

People not knowing, where they are going,
And people just taking their time,
Their random walks are really annoying,
Hurry up, I'm way behind.

> I'm trying to get there faster than you,
> I'm trying to get ahead.
> I've got places to go, and people to do.
> Look out, did ya hear what I said?

People just living without really growing,
And people just marking time,
These mindless souls are really provoking,
Shape up, don't waste your prime.

> I'm trying to get there faster than you,
> I'm trying to get ahead.
> I've got places to go, and people to do.
> Look out, did ya hear what I said?

People just speaking, and not even thinking,
And people not using their minds.
Their senseless gab is really quite boring,
Come on, don't be that kind.

       I'm trying to get there faster than you,
       I'm trying to get ahead.
       I've got places to go, and people to do.
       Look out, did ya hear what I said?

People just looking, without really seeing,
And people not scanning their clime.
These sightless souls are very perplexing,
Look around, are you really that blind?

       I'm trying to get there faster than you,
       I'm trying to get ahead.
       I've got places to go, and people to do.
       Look out, did ya hear what I said?

Sentimental Over You

Let There Be Moonglow

The sun, just down,
Leaves twilight to mute
the red roses,
the yellow willows,
the purple peonies.

In the ensuing dusk,
the full Moon rises
like one more neon sign
over the city.

As it begins its ascent
We stare into the cobalt blue sky
and say,
"What a wonderful night this is."
A lover's Moon you call it.
And you say, "It's a *Bella Notté.*"

The Moon continues its rise.
Is someone in Hollywood filming?
Or, do they have enough full Moons?
Can anyone have enough full Moons?

Reflections in a Double Doo Wop

I drove my love to the airport today.
Her heart now beats *A Thousand Miles Away.*

Over the Mountain, Across the Sea,
We have an *Unchained Melody.*

In the Still of the Night I put music on,
And listen to old doo wop songs.

C, A minor, F, then G,
Set me in a maudlin key.

My heart becomes a little blue.
All I want is *Only You.*

Tears on My Pillow are strange for me.
My *Heart and Soul* need a Chablis.

I should probably change this song.
Perhaps a *Rama Lama, Ding Dong*?

Puppy Love

In our youth
We built sand castles.

Some were strong with moats and walls,
Others were quick attempts to test our finesse.

The tides erased our labors;
The skills we learned live on.

First Star I See Tonight

Thirty minutes early for her plane, I step out of our car
and leave behind the smell of Chicken Tikka Masala.

I walk towards the terminal
to see if UA6693 is on time.

I scan the sky.
One low bright star is shining.
Are the fifty people on UA6693
Represented by that speck of light?

I stare as the star moves closer,
trying to come to grips
with her being in this expanding star.

The light resolves into an airplane,
and streaks past me down the runway.

I walk to the grassy waiting area
as UA6693 pulls to a stop.

The door opens.
The steps come down.
One by one
the passengers get off.
Old ladies needing help down the stairs,
Little kids trying to go down faster than their parent's grip allows.

Passengers string out for the fifty yards
from the plane to the gate.
Yet, she isn't among them.

The interior light of the plane
illuminates the empty portal.
A mother, struggling with a baby in her arms,
steps into the doorway.

Behind them,
silhouetted in the doorway,
my flame patiently waits,
not knowing that the Chicken Tikka Masala
is growing cold.

At the Hop

Grab a partner
Shake, rattle, and roll
Twist and shout
Wipe out
            with
Satisfaction

Then,
Every third dance,
            or so,
The slow ones
Oh, those slow ones.

The magic moments
The unchained melodies
Songs we cherish

We hold each other
Listen to the words
Feel the beat of our hearts

Emotions not understood
Traces of love
Pretending to be adults

For three and half minutes

Once

They held hands at football games
Sat closely on the cold bus rides home

They slow danced at the hops
Shared milkshakes at the Parkway
Laughed over pizza at George's
And ate pork tenderloins at The Igloo

In the summer
They dunked each other at the town pool
And during the rest periods
Coupled daydreams with the clouds' illusions

They were friends

Now they are faded memories
And occasional dreams

The Windy City

She said that I am falling in love with Chicago.
That's a difficult pill to swallow.

I grew up right outside that toddlin' town
when she looked like Eliza Doolittle
still in the gutter,
with a dusty shawl across her broad shoulders.

Oh, she had pretty blossoms to sell,
and wore an interesting hat,
but she didn't entice romance.
Maybe an occasional one night stand.

Like Eliza,
she has washed her face,
put on a new dress,
and now dances with finesse.

I have taken the time to get to know her.
I've stayed over a few nights,
Listened to her sing,
and grown accustomed to her facade.

Still, I use her and run away.
Her ports are convenient.
Her beauty I admire.
But San Francisco is where I left my heart.

Heavy Metal

Five Platinum Coils
Were put in my head
To stop the noise
When I go to bed.

The noise is gone!
And now I hear
The sounds of silence,
Loud and clear.

Let's Go Fly a Kite

In the flying field
Full of milkweed and dandelions
Bounded by the tracks of the Illinois Central,
The muddy Kankakee River,
And Mick's house.

Yet, far enough from home
To be on our own.

As Spring approaches
And the river thaws
We mend our kites with
Sticks salvaged from kite-catching maples
Multi-colored wrapping paper and grocery sacks
Last year's string

For tails
We use our dad's
Garish ties.

The Mobile Gas Station
Gives some of us free kites —
Red horses with wings
To ride high in the sky.

When the April winds blow
Our kites fly.

Old string
Snaps with a gust.
Off to the dime store we scamper,
After begging our parents for a nickel.

Kids from across the river
Join us via the railroad bridge -
A real bad idea
Our parents say.

One of the kids
Shows up with a blue box kite
He spent the winter building -
Elaborate and exotic as it soars,
Fragile when it falls.

We build a lean-to from scavenged wood
To block the wind.
The older boys light a fire
And tell us to watch for adults.

We stake the string to the ground,
Let the kites fly themselves
While we sit in the lean-to
And enjoy our freedom.

Until our parents' whistles
Pull us home.

Getting Sentimental Over You

My old trombone,
Lovingly polished
Until her shine wore off,

Sits on my dresser
Taunting and haunting me
With memories of:

Dad buying her before fifth grade,
Practicing until my thin lips bled,

    Morning rehearsals on the damp football grass,
    A season bewitched by a saxophone playing lass,

        October Friday nights shivering in the stands,
        The teasing twirler who whistled commands,

    Playing *Entrata Festiva* on Easter Sunday,
    Lugging her to school every Monday,

Music camp with Mary Sue,
Marching Michigan Avenue,

    In the pit while *Carousel* and *Pinafore* were groomed,
    Spring rehearsals when tulips and hormones bloomed,

Desires to get my chops back working again,
Dreams to sound like Jack, Tommy, or Glenn.

Boom

Bursting My Bubble

Twenty years after graduating
I am back on the campus
Where I met my wife,
Where I earned my degrees,
Where I learned some social skills.

I walk my old stomping grounds,
The Quad,
      Where we played Frisbee and watched girls.
The Alma Mater,
      Where we took our graduation photos.
Murphy's Pub.
      Where we relaxed on Fridays.

I feel my oats
As if I am still a student again.

A gaggle of undergrads walk past.

I smile.

And … they say,
Hi Pops!

Still Hopeful

"The scientist describes what is; the engineer creates what never was."
— Theodore von Kármán

In 1865, Jules Verne told us we would go to the Moon.
In 1969, we went.

In 1904, Mark Twain told us of the telelectroscope.
Since the 1970s we've had the Internet.

In 1911, Hugo Gernsback wrote of an ether wave reflection.
In 1940, we devised RADAR.

Dick Tracy wore a 2-way wrist radio in 1946.
We now have the Smartwatch.

The Jetsons used a house-cleaning robot.
The Roomba now sweeps our hut.

In *Fahrenheit 451*, Ray Bradbury
Predicted our pervasive earbud headphones.

In 2001, Arthur C. Clarke said we would have the Newspad.
We have the iPad.

HAL 9000 (from Urbana, Illinois) could speak.
My smart phone has a lady's tongue.

Star Trek showed us the communicator
So Scotty could beam us up.

We all now have our mobile phones,
But we still can't be beamed up.

I see nary a hoverboard,
Nor
        A replicator,
        A Hypersonic Jump Drive,
        Or the much needed Flux Capacitor

I want
        My flying car,
        My Teleporter,
        And my very own time machine.

Oh, and
        World Peace.

I Never Stole a Watermelon

I've never pushed over an outhouse, broken my nose, or ridden a horse to school. My dad has. I've never gotten caught playing poker in the back of the school bus, put a firecracker in a mailbox on Halloween, or knocked myself out trying to fly like Superman. My brother has. Not that I'd want to put any of those on my resume, but everything I have done can be put on my resume.

I'm a victim of the year of my birth, 1950, the halfway point in the Twentieth Century. World War I, The Great Depression, Prohibition, and World War II all happened before I was born. I entered the world right when it was getting ready to rest. The main menace to the U.S. when I was a kid was rock and roll. My development was guided by *Father Knows Best*, *Make Room for Daddy*, and *Leave it to Beaver*.

Remember the song "Will My Dog be Proud of Me"? I can still sing it. All my life I've wondered if my dog would approve of my actions and my dog, Dixie, tiptoed around mud puddles. So, because of Howdy Doody, my social life was about as exciting as ditch water.

I never went to a canal party where you drink beer, go skinny dipping (sometimes with girls), and tell lots of lies about it at school on Monday. I did go to school on Mondays.

I never dated until I was sixteen and never drove a car until I was legal. When my dad was a kid, you could drive as soon as your feet reached the pedals on the Model A, and, of course, you were in the field driving the tractor (or was it oxen?) as soon as you could walk.

I can't tell locker room stories — I didn't play sports. I can tell you about all the heavy action that goes on in the trombone section at band practice. Well, no, I guess I can't. I was the one who paid attention to the director.

I can't tell war stories because the only uniforms I ever wore were Boy Scout and band uniforms. My dad was a fighter pilot and my great granddad helped Sherman burn Atlanta, so I know I have it in my genes.

I got a college deferment for Vietnam. Not that I wanted to go to Nam, but they say R & R was great. I have a friend who admired a girl's puppy in Bangkok so she gave it to him - with rice and hot sauce.

I have never broken a bone. I have a friend who tells about ending upside down in the fork of a tree on a ski slope in Aspen with two broken legs. Another friend broke both his arms in Karate class. Even my wife managed to break her leg by riding her bike behind a neighbor as he pulled out of his drive. My daughter broke her arm when she was only five. And did I tell you how my dad broke his nose?

I've never done anything cool. The people who wrote the Boy Scout Handbook point to me with pride. I've learned the fine art of living vicariously. I can tell if a person has a good story by looking at the glow in her cheeks or the bend in his nose. I've heard some of the best whiskey drinking, girl chasing, plane flying, car racing, bootlegging stories ever told. In fact, I have this friend who tells a whiskey drinking, girl chasing, plane flying, car racing, bootlegging story that would curl your hair.

Ok, ok. I did do some crazy things. I invented streaking! I escaped from my bath and ran naked down the street when I was three. In fifth grade I got sent to the principal's office for allegedly pushing Barbara Marshall into a mud puddle. I hustled pool in college. Well, actually I helped my friend, Ambrose, the Big Ten pocket billiards champion, hustle by being his shill. The biggie is - I snuck into a strip joint and drank beer at the University of Wisconsin when I was only nineteen. I even talked to one of the strippers. A really nice girl, Bubbles I think her name was. She showed me what to do with a dollar bill.

The Stained Glass Window

Multicolored glass
Held together by threads of lead
Depicts myths and scenes
Of someone else's dreams.

An explosion of life
Breaks the static tableau
Casting shards of colored glass
To my feet.

I gather the attractive pieces;
Pour them into a Pringles can;
Add reflective surfaces;
And make a kaleidoscope.

I twist it and turn it
Study the patterns
To find those that
Resonate with my soul.

I break open the can
Pour the bits and pieces on the table
Make a mosaic of patterns
That ring true.

I add some dichroic glass,
Build my own window,
Bind it with mercury instead of lead
And leave the images unframed.

Lessons in Relativity

Today will be yesterday,
　　Tomorrow.

Tonight will be last night,
　　In the morning.

This Sunday will be last Sunday
　　On Tuesday.

The yell will be an echo
　　In a shake.

"In a while" will be "We did that"
　　Before you know it.

The river always flows past the pier
　　But never the same water.

The Things My Dad Taught Me

Whether you do a job for gratis or for pay,
do the best you are capable of doing.

When speaking in public remember two things:
      Say what you have to say and then shut up.
      Make sure your zipper is up.

A man can't get any serious fishin' done
if he takes his girlfriend along.

When buying tools,
you get what you pay for.

People watching is great sport.

Tuck your shirt in when out in public.

If you are not five minutes early,
you are late.

Always, take your hat off when you go into a building;
There are no exceptions to this rule.

Keep your hair cut short and
people won't notice you are bald.

Study hard,
relax when you can,
and take advantage of the opportunities offered you.

Good friends are hard to come by.
Treasure them.

Life is too short even if you live to be nearly 95.

Boom

Mickey Mouse Club, Hoola Hoop, Etch A Sketch
Howdy Doody, Silly Putty, Hound Dog
Mr. Ed, Father Knows Best, Rin Tin Tin
I Love Lucy, Stan the Man, Super Balls

Sputnik, Woodstock, To Kill a Mockingbird
White Rabbit, Annie Hall, Blow Up, Psycho
Star Wars, Dr. No, Zip Codes, Apollo
Cara Mia, Michelle, Fool on the Hill

Born to Be Wild, Ring of Fire, Stand by Me
Watergate, Assassinate, In Cold Blood
Kent State, Bay of Pigs, We Shall Overcome
Vietnam, Berlin Wall, Give Peace a Chance

Walk on the Wild Side, When I'm Sixty-Four
Let It Be, In-A-Gadda-Da-Vida

Postscript

A Question of Resonance

After you spend
Hours,
Days,
Even weeks
Writing and tweaking a poem,
If only one person
Finds it resonant,
Is it a success,
Or a failure?

Internal Dialogue #2

So, what do you think now?   … asked the poet.
It's hard! … said the engineer.

Oh, and integro-differential equations aren't?
Well, that's different.

How?
Life gets in the way of writing.

But it's life you are writing about.
I kind of figured that out.

What else did you learn?
Poems work best if you read them out loud.

What about that emotion thing?
I was taught that there should be "No public display of emotion."

So …You never laugh out loud?
It's easy to hide behind humor.

True.
But what if the reader thinks the poems are about me?

They won't. They'll see their own lives first.
Maybe, but won't they be scared of the ambiguity?

Ambiguity is what life is all about.
Hmmm.

Notes

I personally like to hear the back stories of writings I have read so I have added a few notes about some of my musings and poems. Since many of the writings are anecdotal, I make no comments on those. If your favorite is not here, buy me a drink and ask me about it.

Internal Dialogue #1
In my very first writing class which was taught by the Edgar Award winning author Dennis Lynds (Michael Collins), we were reading each other's works and commenting on them. We had just read what I call a slice of life story and, as a thirty-year-old engineer, I stated that I didn't get it. Dennis looked at me and said, "You're not supposed to get it, Mike, you're supposed to feel it."

The Wolf Moon
This is the first free-verse poem I ever wrote. It was begun in January 2011 and started as a set of emails between me and my Executive Assistant, Joy Hurnblad, while I was on the long boring bus ride from O'Hare Airport to Urbana, Illinois, during a Wolf Moon.

To A Hoppy Toad
My maternal Grandma, Dessie Shearer, really could take warts off with a bean, an apron, and an incantation.

A Turtle in a Tree
My attempt at tipping this cat's hat to Dr. Seuss.

The Nature of Things
This stems from the haunting image that is ingrained in my mind of a dead deer I saw in Rocky Mountain National Park on our honeymoon.

Orange Is an Easy Rhyme
Don't ever tell an engineer that something can't be done.

Puppy Love
This originally was a six page short story. I condensed it.

Boom
Writing this quasi-sonnet was fun for me. I now have twenty pages of lists of things (toys, TV shows, movies, songs, inventions, events) that impacted me in the first thirty years of my life. This, also, is the only poem I have ever written with alternate endings depending on my mood. They are:

> *Dizzy, With a Little Help from My Friends*
> *They're Coming To Take Me Away, Ha-Haaa!*

or

> *Staying Alive, I Want to Hold Your Hand*
> *Dang Me, You've Made Me So Very Happy*

Additional Note:
Versions of the following originally appeared in my Blog – "Dogged Dialogues, Diatribes, and Doggerel" at http://doggeddoggerel. blogspot.com/.

The Wolf Moon
Moon Shadow
A Noisy Thanks
I Never Stole a Watermelon,
Reflections in a Double Doo Wop, and
Petit Gris

Acknowledgements

John Donne famously wrote, "No Man is an Island" in his Mediation XVII and that is certainly true when one is trying to produce anything creative. Hence, there are many people whom I wish to thank and acknowledge.

Firstly, I have to thank my parents, my wife, and my children who have never rolled their eyes, too much, when I speak of writing poetry. I also need to thank all the writing teachers I have had over time. In particular I want to thank Jim Lowers who, besides being one of my high school English teachers, greatly encouraged me a few years ago when I decided to try to write poems. I also want to thank Mrs. Larson, my high school college prep English teacher, who irritated me so much that I had an itch that I finally had to scratch. Dennis Lynds (Michael Collins) was my first writing teacher and taught me an amazing amount. I have also had the good fortune of attending the Santa Barbara Writer's Conference (SBWC) on several occasions and all of the teachers I have had there have been very instrumental in teaching me craft. Lisa Lenard-Cook and Matt Pallamary both are not only great teachers but also have been very supportive to a neophyte writer. Also, the poetry teachers at SBWC- Perie Longo, David Starkey, and Christopher Buckley- have helped me sharpen whatever craft I may have up to this point.

I must thank my friends who have read much of the work in this collection, commented on it and have been exceptionally supportive. This list includes Frank Bouxsein, Kathy Callahan-Howell, Joy Hurnblad, Anita Merriman, Janie Jerch, and Christa Deacy-Quinn.

Thanks to Maddie Rose Maranto who executed the art, the layout, and the design of this book.

Finally, my wife, Pam, has edited everything I have ever written thus keeping me from looking like the C-level English student that I really am.

About the Author

M.L. VanBlaricum, better known as Mike, Pops, Daddy, Grandpa, and Duckman, unless he is in trouble and then he is invariably called Michael, lives in Santa Barbara, California, and Urbana, Illinois, with his wife, Pam. He was educated in public schools in Momence and Princeton, Illinois, and at the University of Illinois at Urbana-Champaign where he received three degrees in Electrical Engineering. He has been a Kool-Aid and an earthworm salesman, a paperboy, a lawn mower, a lifeguard, a deliveryman, a musician, a steel worker, a house painter, an appliance repairman, a Boy Scout, a ballet dancer, a lead smelter, a printer's assistant, a Girl Scout leader, a collector of books, a rare book dealer, a columnist, an author, a lecturer, a research engineer, an inventor, and a CEO.

Manufactured by Amazon.ca
Bolton, ON

35290115R00057